Folk Tales
from
Portugal

Folk Tales
from
Portugal

Alan S. Feinstein

Illustrated by Diana L. Paxson

South Brunswick and New York: A. S. Barnes and Company
London: Thomas Yoseloff Ltd

A. S. Barnes and Co., Inc.
Cranbury, New Jersey 08512

Thomas Yoseloff Ltd
108 New Bond Street
London W1Y OQX, England

Library of Congress Cataloging in Publication Data

Feinstein, Alan S
  Folk Tales from Portugal.
    SUMMARY: Eighteen folk tales from Portugal about
good and evil, the wise and the foolish.
    1. Tales, Portuguese. [1. Folklore—Portugal]
I. Paxson, Diana L., illus. II. Title.
PZ8.1.F26Fm   398.2′09469   74-146754
ISBN 0-498-01031-7

Printed in the United States of America

TO MY DAUGHTER

Contents

Acknowledgment

My sincere appreciation to Miss Mary Silva for her translating assistance that helped make this book possible.

Folk Tales
from
Portugal

The Boys
and the Donkey

There once were two boys who wanted a donkey.
So very, very much . . .

In one of the many villages in Portugal there once lived
two boys by the names of Victor and Manuel. They
were both ten years old.

Like the other boys in the village they were neither
very bad nor very good. They were just ordinary boys,
like most boys everywhere.

But unlike boys in other lands, every boy in this village
had the same desire—to have a donkey. For they all had
the responsibility of feeding their family's cows, which
meant that each boy had to take his cows out to the
fields to graze every morning before going to school and
bring them back on his way home every afternoon.
Except for the few lucky boys who had donkeys: they
could take their donkeys to the fields and load them up
with enough grass in a single trip to keep their cows fed
for days at a time. So you can see why every boy in this
village who didn't have a donkey wanted one more than
anything else in the world.

Now, there happened to be an old man who lived in

this village who once in a great while let some of the boys use his donkey—if they asked him very nicely and if he was in a good mood when they asked.

Both Victor and Manuel had asked him many times if they could use his donkey. But they had never been lucky enough to get him to say yes. Oh, how they wished they had a donkey like that to use whenever they wanted. In fact, they were saving every *centavo*[1] they could get in hopes of some day having enough money to be able to buy donkeys of their own. But *centavos* were so hard to come by. The weeks and months passed and their savings hardly seemed to grow.

Well, one Sunday after church, Victor and Manuel decided to ask the old man if he would please let them use his donkey that afternoon. What a pleasure if just once they could have the donkey so as to be able to gather and bring back a big load of grass. Then they would not have to bother with the cows for a whole week. So they went to the old man's house and asked him as politely as they could. But they had no more luck this time than they had ever had before.

"No, go away," barked the old man. "Don't bother me!"

Some boys had disturbed him by playing ball near his house last evening and he had been in a bad mood because of it all day.

Victor and Manuel were very disappointed. It seemed they would never get to borrow the old man's donkey.

The next day when Victor and Manuel arrived at school, everybody was talking about some shocking news—the old man's donkey had been stolen. When he

_____
1. A penny.

had gone out to his yard to feed his donkey that morning, the donkey was nowhere to be found.

"Imagine that!" gasped Victor. "One of the boys must have taken him."

"Yes, but who?" wondered Manuel.

"Let's ask the boys after school," declared Victor.

"That's a good idea," agreed Manuel.

So after school they began questioning their friends. But before long Manuel said it was time for him to get his cows. Nobody they had questioned so far seemed to know anything about the missing donkey.

"We'll ask more of the boys tomorrow," said Victor.

"Fine," agreed Manuel. And they bid each other goodbye.

The next day after school they began questioning boys again. But before long Manuel said he had to get his cows. And none of the boys they had questioned so far seemed to know any more about the missing donkey than the boys they had questioned yesterday.

Every day that week after school Victor and Manuel asked everybody they could if they knew where the old man's donkey was. But nobody seemed to know. Finally Victor and Manuel had asked everyone in the school, without any success. The donkey was still missing, and nobody seemed to have the slightest idea where he was.

Victor wanted to go into the village to ask more people. But Manuel didn't. "I have to get the cows," he said. So he left.

"That's strange," Victor said to his other friends. "Manuel left early every day this week. He never used to leave so early before to get his cows home. I'm going to follow him," he decided. So he did.

Manuel didn't go to the fields for his cows. Instead he turned off the main road and hurried into the hills. And Victor followed right after him.

Then, lo and behold, Manuel led Victor straight to the donkey. There he was, tied to a tree behind some bushes.

Manuel stroked the donkey's head and took a carrot from his pocket which he had brought for him. Then Victor stepped out in front of them. "Now I know who took the old man's donkey," he said.

Manuel hung his head.

"We have to return him," declared Victor.

"Yes, I know," murmured Manuel.

So Victor and Manuel led the donkey back to the old man's house. And you can imagine how delighted the old man was to see his donkey again.

Manuel admitted to the old man that he had been the one who had taken the donkey and he was very sorry for it. He also declared that he had been afraid to even use the donkey for fear somebody might see them and that he had been worried sick over the bad thing he had done by taking him.

"Serves you right," growled the old man. "Now get out of my house. And don't you ever dare to come back!"

Then he turned to Victor and thanked him. "I heard how hard you were trying all week to find my donkey. And you finally did. As your reward you may use him from now on whenever you wish."

Which made Victor very happy. At last he had a donkey to use to get grass for his cows.

Of course he would also use him to get grass for Manuel's cows, too. Didn't good friends always help one another?

Why, it was almost as if they had planned it that way.

Manuel stroked the donkey's head and took a carrot from
his pocket which he had brought for him.

The Farmer and His Three Farms

There were these very smart workers.
At least they thought they were . . .

There once was a rich farmer who had three farms. When the time came to harvest the wheat he called all his field hands together and told them to go to his first farm and do the harvesting. So off they went.

But when the field hands reached the first farm they sat down in the shade under the trees to rest a bit before beginning their labors. All except for one field hand by the name of Alfredo. The other farm hands knew that Alfredo was not so smart as they were; he would never think of resting before beginning work. No, not Alfredo. He was foolish enough to start work right away while all the other field hands were having a rest. And even when they did finally manage to join him in work they did a lot more chatting to one another than anything else. But not Alfredo. Foolish Alfredo kept right on working as hard as he could.

When the farmer arrived he was anything but pleased with what he found. Much of the wheat had been rag-

They sat down in the shade under the trees to rest a bit before beginning their labors.

gedly cut at uneven lengths and sloppily stacked. Part of the field hadn't even been done yet.

"Who's responsible for this terrible job of harvesting?" he asked his field hands grimly.

Of course, none of them wanted to take the blame. And they knew just who to give it to. They pointed at Alfredo.

"He is," they said.

Poor Alfredo didn't know what to say. So he said nothing.

The farmer was very angry.

"Go harvest the second farm," he told them. "And be sure you do a better job on that one!"

When they arrived at the second farm, the same thing happened there as had happened at the first farm. All the workers except Alfredo sat down under the shade of the trees to rest and when they finally did get to work they did very little indeed. Alfredo worked as hard and as fast as he could to make up for them but he couldn't do the work of them all. And when the farmer arrived to see what had been done, the results of the harvesting that greeted him were no better than they had been at the first farm.

"Who's responsible for this?" he thundered.

"Alfredo is," said the wily field hands.

Poor Alfredo didn't know what to say. So he said nothing.

"Go harvest the third farm!" the farmer ordered them angrily. "And do a decent job of it this time if you know what's good for you. Do you understand?"

All the workers nodded. But when they arrived at the third farm their laziness again got the best of them. That is, except for Alfredo. While his fellow workers rested under the trees he worked as hard and as fast as he could. Even when the others did get to work they were too busy talking and joking most of the time to be of much use. Poor Alfredo worked as hard and as fast as possible but the harvesting was far too much for one man with so little help from the others. And when the farmer arrived he found that this farm had been no better harvested than his other two had been.

The farmer was furious. "Who did this!" he roared.

"Alfredo did," came the answer.

Again poor Alfredo didn't know what to say.

The farmer stamped angrily off, leaving the field hands smiling to themselves, thinking how clever they were. Not only had they escaped a hard day's work but they had managed to escape the blame as well.

But on pay day they were in for a surprise. When they went to collect their pay there was no money for them, not a single *centavo*. That is, except for Alfredo. He received quite a lot of money.

"What's going on here?" exclaimed some of the field hands to the farmer. "How come we got no money and Alfredo got so much?"

"Yes, how come?" demanded others. "Alfredo was the one who did such a terrible job on the harvesting, not us."

"Yes, that's right," chimed in the rest.

"That may be true," said the farmer. "But you couldn't expect him to do a good job of harvesting three farms by himself. And since you all seemed to agree he did it by himself he certainly deserves your pay as well as his own. And that's just what he got."

There was nothing the field hands could say. They realized they had trapped themselves—they were not so smart as they had thought.

As for Alfredo, it was possible he was actually smarter than them all. He had kept his mouth shut and let his actions speak for him instead. This had turned out to be a very smart thing to do indeed. Alfredo had his pockets full of money to prove it.

The Man Who Never Smiled

Meet a man who never smiled—
Well, almost never . . .

Once upon a time there was a man by the name of Mr. Lima who bought some property in the country near the sea. Now, it so happens that every family in this area had a vineyard with several grapevines in it from which they made wine. And there was a vineyard on the property Mr. Lima had bought too.

During the spring and summer months each family would tend its vineyard with loving care, for everyone wanted to be sure of having delicious wine in the fall.

The people would inspect their grapevines every day and smile happily at one another. "It won't be long now before they're ripe," some would say.

And others would smile and answer back: "No, it won't be long now."

The very next morning after Mr. Lima had moved in he went out to his vineyard to begin tending to his grapevines too.

"It won't be long now before they're ripe," neighbors were saying to one another with a smile.

"No, it won't be long now," others were smiling in answer.

23

Then some of Mr. Lima's neighbors noticed him. "It won't be long now before they're ripe," they greeted him with a smile.

"That's true," said Mr. Lima. But Mr. Lima didn't smile.

The neighbors were shocked. Why, everybody in the area always greeted one another with a smile. For as long as they could remember. Didn't all wine makers always smile?

The next morning when they came out of their houses, they greeted each other again.

"It won't be long now before they're ripe," some said with a smile.

"No, it won't be long now," others answered with a smile.

Mr. Lima came out to tend to his vineyard.

"It won't be long now before they're ripe," his neighbors greeted him with a smile.

"That's right," nodded Mr. Lima. But Mr. Lima didn't smile.

The news of the unsmiling Mr. Lima spread fast and far. Soon everybody in the countryside had heard about him.

"Imagine, a wine maker who doesn't smile," they said to one another. "What a miserable man he must be."

People went out of their way to greet him, to see for themselves. And, sure enough, no matter how pleasant or cheerful they were to him, it made no difference— Mr. Lima never smiled.

"Old stone face," they began calling him behind his back. And the name stuck.

With the coming of September, the grapes ripened and were soon ready to be picked. Happy and laughing, the people gathered their grapes into baskets and brought them to little wine shacks they had on a hillside over-looking the sea. Except for Mr. Lima. Oh, yes, he gath-ered his grapes and brought them to a little wine shack he had too on the hillside overlooking the sea. But Mr. Lima never smiled.

Then the people began to crush the grapes to make the wine, laughing and singing and happy as could be. Except for Mr. Lima who went about crushing his grapes as stone faced as ever. But the others were too joyous to pay him the slightest attention.

"This is the day we wait every year for!" cried one of the wine makers, filling a cup with wine.

"How true, how true," sang another, filling his cup too.

And all the men and women and even the children filled their cups with the wine and drank and laughed and frolicked. Except for Mr. Lima. He just took a little taste of his wine and smacked his lips with pleasure. But he still didn't smile.

The others refilled their cups. And then refilled them again. And the hillside rang with their merriment and song. Dancing and singing and drinking they had a won-derful night.

But not Mr. Lima. He just sat by himself near his wine shack. Without so much as a smile.

When the other wine makers were through with their revelry they were so exhausted that they went to sleep right where they were, on the ground by their shacks. The next morning when they awoke, they rubbed the sleep from their eyes and began to clean up.

"Any wine left?" somebody asked.

"None here," came an answer.

"Nor here," came another.

One by one everybody answered that they had drunk all their wine.

The people sighed in disappointment.

"I'd give anything for a drink right now," said one.

"So would I," said another.

To which they all agreed, as they did every year the morning after their wine-making celebration.

"Well, nothing to do now but wait until next year," they sighed. And, with that, they began to trudge back to their homes.

Suddenly one of them noticed Mr. Lima by his shack.

"Look, there's Mr. Lima," he said.

"Look at all the bottles of wine he's got!" said another.

Sure enough, everybody could see the bottles of wine which Mr. Lima had made from his grapes the night before.

"He didn't even drink a single glass of his wine last night," remarked one of the wine makers. "He has it all left."

"It's the only wine around," murmured another. "Think how valuable it is."

"Imagine how much he could sell it for," everybody realized.

Mr. Lima must have heard them. He smiled.

Mr. Lima must have heard them. He smiled.

The Two Beggars

Sometimes bad people aren't punished by others—
They punish themselves . . .

In the woods on one of the islands of Portugal lived a group of beggars. They all had different things wrong with them, except for a few who just pretended to have something wrong because they found it easier to beg than to work.

Every day they would go into the villages and towns, begging from house to house.

"Help a poor beggar!" they would cry. "Have pity on a man! Help a poor beggar!"

And, indeed, many of the people would take pity on them and give them money or food. In fact, many of the beggars got more from begging than many good people got from working hard all day long.

Now, one of the most successful beggars was a man who was blind. Some people said that he had lost his sight because he had been a bad man. But whether or not that was true, the fact is that he was a very bad man indeed.

Another of the beggars was a boy who had no family. Some people said that he had lost his family because he had been a bad boy. But whether or not that was true, the fact is that he was a very bad boy indeed.

This blind man and this boy always went begging together. For with somebody to guide him the blind man could get around to more houses, thus increasing his chances to get more food and money. So he wanted the boy with him. And the boy wanted to be with the blind man because he knew that people were more likely to give to him if he was with a blind man than if he were begging by himself. So you can understand why they stayed together.

However this doesn't mean that they had any love for each other. Oh, no. The fact is that none of the beggars could trust one another. And the blind man and the boy trusted each other least of all.

Nevertheless every day they would put on their shabbiest clothes and go begging from house to house together.

"Help a poor blind man!" the blind beggar would cry out. "Have pity! Help a poor blind man!"

"Yes, help a poor blind man and a poor beggar boy!" begged the little boy. "Have pity on us! Help a poor blind man and a poor beggar boy!"

And some people did take pity on them and gave them a coin or two or some bread. And once in a while some very kind person even gave them a piece of cheese.

The boy would take everything and put it in a big sack which he always carried with him. Then, at the end of the day, the beggar boy and the blind man would return to the woods and divide their take, being very careful not to let the other beggars steal any of it from them.

And, of course, they had to be most careful of one another. For each would steal from the other whenever he could. Many times the boy would try to keep the choicest pieces of bread and cheese for himself and many times the blind man would demand bigger portions and threaten to beat the boy to get them. And often the boy would try to keep more money than was his share while just as often the blind man would demand more money for himself and threaten to whip the boy to get that too.

Now, it so happened that one evening as they went off to a secluded corner of the woods to divide their day's take, there was a particularly nice piece of cheese among the food they had received.

"Let's divide up the cheese we got first," said the blind man, his mouth watering for it.

"All right," said the boy. So he took out the cheese from their sack and cut off a small piece and gave it to the blind man, keeping the big piece for himself.

The blind man sniffed the piece of cheese the boy had given him. "This doesn't smell like half the cheese," he said. (For he had a very keen sense of smell.) "You are trying to cheat me!"

"Oh, no, I'm not," said the boy, dropping the big piece of cheese behind a tree.

The blind man sniffed at his piece of cheese again. "You lie!" he roared. "This is only a tiny piece of the cheese we got!" And throwing it down in anger he began beating the boy with his cane.

"Help, help!" cried the boy, trying to dodge the blows.

But the blind man's hearing was so sharp that he could hear just where the boy was moving and followed right after him, still beating him and shouting: "Trying to cheat me, eh? Now give me all of the cheese—all of it, do you hear?"

"Help!" cried the boy, still trying in vain to dodge the

And dropping their sack he rolled on the ground, laughing as if he would never stop.

blind man's blows. But he didn't want to give up the big piece of cheese. Suddenly he had an idea.

"Watch out!" he yelled. "There's a brook here—jump!"

When the blind man heard this he immediately jumped to avoid the water. But there was no water. There was only a big tree and the blind man jumped right into it and banged his head.

"OW!" he screamed.

The boy laughed and laughed. "Serves you right, you old fool!" And dropping their sack he rolled on the ground, laughing as if he would never stop.

"Oh, you devil, you little devil!" raged the blind man.

And while the blind man was roaring and the boy was rolling in laughter, some of the other beggars sneaked up on them and stole their sack.

When the blind man and the boy finally stopped roaring and laughing they found that their sack with their food and money were gone. Even the two pieces of cheese they had dropped had been stolen by the other beggars too.

There was nothing they could do except go to sleep with empty pockets and empty stomachs as well. All they had left was each other. Which is just what they deserved.

The Ambitious Pigeon

Ambition is a wonderful thing—
Unless it's carried too far . . .

Once upon a time there were several pigeons who lived in a pigeon coop. Their owner rented them as couriers to carry messages but they were never worked too hard and always had plenty of food and water. So, all in all, they were quite content.

That is, except for one pigeon. He was a very ambitious fellow and yearned to become the courier for the King. And the more he thought about it, the more his yearning grew. He began to look down on his carefree, peaceful existence and chafe at his dull life. His unhappiness grew and grew. Finally, one day when he was out with the other pigeons exercising his wings, he decided there was no better time than right then to re-make his destiny. So he suddenly zoomed away from his companions and headed for the King's palace.

When he reached his destination he alighted on a nearby tree and waited for the King's courier to appear. Sure enough, in a few hours the King's pigeon emerged from a palace window on his way to deliver a message. The ambitious pigeon stayed where he was, waiting for

him to return. And, when he reappeared, the ambitious
pigeon flew into the air behind him and followed him
right through a window of the palace and into his cage
which was in the King's bedchamber.

Now, when the King came to his room and saw two
pigeons in the cage he was quite surprised. Each pigeon
claimed that he was the real courier and since both of
them were about the same size and coloring, the King
couldn't tell which was his.

"Dear me, this is an awful predicament," he exclaimed.
"You both look so much alike I can't tell one from the
other."

So he called his Prime Minister to ask him if he could
tell which was the real courier. But the Prime Minister
couldn't tell either. So the King called all his guards and
asked them. But none of them could tell either.

"Well then, we will just have to hold a contest to see
which pigeon is the fastest," said the King. For the fastest
one would certainly have to be his real courier, he as-
sumed. So he commanded them to both race to the sea
and then return.

The two pigeons took off, flying as fast as they could.
But before reaching the sea the ambitious pigeon sud-
denly turned around and began racing back to the palace.
Naturally he was the first to return.

"Ah, this must be my real courier," said the King.

"No, no—he's not!" cried the real courier, coming
through the window a moment later. "He cheated. He
didn't fly all the way to the sea."

"I did so," lied the ambitious pigeon.

"You did not!" squawked the King's courier.

"Did so!" insisted the imposter.

"Did not!" squawked the real courier.

That evening, while the King was at dinner, the Prime Minister entered the King's bedchamber . . .

"Stop arguing," demanded the King. "I have made my decision." And the King's real courier was banished to the dungeon.

The ambitious pigeon was delighted. At last he was the King's courier as he had always dreamed of being. And he was determined to be the best King's courier there ever was.

That evening, while the King was at dinner, the Prime Minister entered the King's bedchamber and strapped a message tube around the ambitious pigeon's leg.

"Fly to the woods," he told him, "and wait at the foot of the highest tree until this message is picked up."

Anxious to begin his duties and show how well he could do them, the ambitious pigeon immediately started forth on his mission. As soon as he flew out of the window one of the King's guards saw him and notified the King.

"So he was the imposter after all," said the King. "Good riddance to him. He will be long punished for his trickery." And he immediately called for his real courier to be restored to its rightful position.

As for the imposter, when he reached the woods he quickly found the tallest tree and flew down to the base of it. There he waited, intent upon carrying out his instructions as best as any King's courier could, by waiting right there as he had been told to do until his message was picked up. What he did not know was that the message tube around his leg contained nothing, that it had just been placed there to determine whether or not he was truly the King's real courier. For the King's real courier would never carry a message from anybody but the King.

Often the pigeons with whom he had once lived would think of him when they flew over the palace.

"He must be the King's courier by now without a doubt," they would say.

"That's what comes of having ambition like his," they would add. "Oh, what important things he must be doing."

As for the ambitious pigeon he just sat at the foot of the tall tree in the woods and waited and waited. He was still sitting and waiting long after everyone at the palace had forgotten all about him.

The Old Man and His Grandson

Never, never try to please everyone—
Or look what can happen . . .

Many years ago there lived a man and a donkey. They had been together a long time and had grown old. Now, this old man had a grandson of whom he was very fond. He knew he did not have much longer to live and wished he could leave his grandson something of value. But all he had was his old donkey.

One day he called his grandson to his side and asked if he would like to take a trip with him to the market place.

"I am going there to sell my donkey," said the old man. "I am too old to be taking any more crops to market so I won't be needing him. And, old as he is, this donkey still has a few good years left."

The grandson readily agreed to go with them.

"But let's not ride on the donkey though," declared the old man. "It is a hot day and a long journey to the market place. We can spare him our weight by using our feet."

So the grandson jumped on. And they continued along.

So they started out on the road to the market place, walking alongside the donkey.

On the way they came upon some farmers working in the fields by the roadside.

"Look at that mean old man," the farmers said to one another. "On a hot day like this he makes that poor lad walk instead of letting him ride in comfort on the donkey. Isn't that a shame?"

Upon hearing this the old man stopped and had his grandson get on the donkey. Then they continued their journey.

About an hour later they came upon some more farmers working in their fields by the roadside.

"Look at that young rascal astride the donkey," the farmers said to one another. "He rides while that poor old man has to walk alongside them. What do you think of that? The old man should be resting his tired bones on the donkey's back, not the youngster."

On hearing this the old man stopped the donkey and bid his grandson to get down. Then the old man got astride the donkey. And they started on again.

They had almost reached their destination when they met a crowd of people on their way back from the market place.

"Look at that shrewd old man," they muttered to one another. "He rides atop the donkey in comfort while he makes the little boy walk. Oh, what a mean old man he must be."

Upon hearing this the old man stopped the donkey and bid his grandson to get on the donkey behind him. So the grandson jumped on. And they continued along.

Soon they approached the entrance to the market place. There were many people here, coming and going, and the traffic was moving very slowly. The old man and his grandson steered the donkey into the line waiting to get into the market place. And there they waited too.

As they did, many people nearby noticed them and began exchanging angry glances—then angry words.

"Look at that cruel pair," they grumbled to one another. "Both of them riding on that poor donkey. Why, they could cripple him with their weight! If they had any sense they would be using their own feet for support rather than forcing that old donkey to carry them." And several of them began to shout at the old man and his grandson how inhuman they were.

The old man and his grandson quickly got down off the donkey. And the menacing crowd withdrew.

"I hope you learned something from this," the old man said to his grandson after the crowd was gone. "When you try to please everybody you end up pleasing nobody. For no matter what you do, some people are bound to think you should have done otherwise. So when you have a decision to make, don't think of pleasing. Do what you think is right."

The grandson had learned a valuable lesson. And he was determined to remember it.

And he did. In fact, it is said that as he grew up he became admired by many for his strong-mindedness and resolve—and he lived a respected and prosperous life.

Meanwhile it is also said that the old man never did sell his donkey that day, that the two of them spent many happy years together before they finally passed on. Why the old man didn't sell his donkey nobody really knows. Perhaps he asked more money for him than anyone wanted to pay. But perhaps he had never really intended to sell him in the first place. After all, such a long time companion who could help teach such a powerful lesson might be considered too valuable to sell at any price.

The Foxes and the Hen House

There once was a family of foxes—
Very, very hungry and very, very smart . . .

Once upon a time there was a family of foxes that lived
near a farm. Now, foxes were known far and wide as being the most cunning of all animals. And these foxes were
no different from their relatives.

But hunting had been very poor for this fox family
lately. Cunning as they were, they could find hardly anything to eat, and as a result they were almost always
hungry.

Now, it so happens that at this nearby farm there was
a hen house. And foxes love hens. But the farmer knew
this, too, and he was determined that no foxes would ever
get to his hens. Oh, no, no fox was ever going to outsmart
him . . . He guarded his hens every day with the eyes of
an eagle. And every evening he made sure that the hen
house was tightly locked and secure before he went to
sleep. And right by his bed he kept a shotgun filled with
buckshot just in case those foxes might dare to try anything during the night.

Well, Mr. and Mrs. Fox had no desire to ever challenge

the farmer and his shotgun so they kept well away from the hen house. But, as the days passed, their little ones became hungrier and hungrier. And so did they. Finally Mr. and Mrs. Fox decided that they simply had to get into that hen house to catch themselves a few hens.

After discussing how they could possibly accomplish their goal, they came to the conclusion that the best way was to try digging a hole under the hen house. So they sneaked down to it one night and began looking for a good spot to dig.

But the farmer had thought they might try something like that and had taken the precaution of planting big rocks all around the hen house. And they were so heavy that Mr. and Mrs. Fox couldn't move any one of them so much as an inch.

Then Mr. Fox spotted a space between two of the rocks that seemed a bit larger than the spaces between the other rocks. It was not enough room for him to get through, even considering how thin from hunger he had become, but when he pointed it out to Mrs. Fox, who was much smaller than he was, she felt she just might be able to squeeze through it.

Of course, realizing the danger involved, Mr. Fox would have preferred to be the one to try but he was too big. So it was agreed that Mrs. Fox would have to do the job.

As quietly as she could Mrs. Fox began scooping dirt out from between the two rocks while Mr. Fox kept a sharp watch. Soon Mrs. Fox had dug a hole beneath the rocks leading under the hen house.

Then she took a deep breath and tried to squeeze herself between the two rocks and into the hole. She squeezed and squeezed as hard as she could. Finally she made it! A moment later she had dashed through the hole and into the hen house.

She was so hungry that she grabbed the first hen she saw and ate her in two swallows. Then she grabbed for another and began eating her too.

But the other hens had set up such a squawking and screeching as soon as they had seen Mrs. Fox that they had awaken the farmer. He grabbed for his gun and came running.

Mrs. Fox heard him coming. But the two hens she had eaten had made her stomach so big that she couldn't even get back into the hole she had dug, let alone hope to squeeze by the rocks. All she could do was what she had been taught a long time ago if she ever found herself in such a situation—play dead. And that's just what she did. She stretched out on the floor, let herself go limp and didn't move a muscle.

The farmer came bursting into the hen house.

"Ah, ha!" he cried, spotting Mrs. Fox on the floor. "Thought you could outsmart me—thought you could get my hens, did you? Now you'll pay!" And he aimed his shotgun right at her heart.

But Mrs. Fox didn't move so much as a muscle.

The farmer tightened his finger on the trigger. Then he hesitated. This fox seemed to be already dead.

Very cautiously he edged toward her, still keeping his gun trained on her in case this was a trick.

He stood right over her. Mrs. Fox didn't move.

Then he kicked her. Mrs. Fox still didn't move.

The farmer noticed her tongue hanging out and her eyes glassy as death. She didn't seem to have a breath of life in her.

He bent down and picked her up by the tail. Then he

She suddenly put on a burst of speed and fled for the woods.

shook her violently back and forth. And she gave no sign
of having any more life than before.

"Frightened to death, eh?" laughed the farmer. "I don't
even have to waste any buckshot on you. I'll just bury you
good and deep. And good riddance!"

So he carried her out behind his garden, dropped her
on the ground and began digging a grave.

But as soon as he put her down she sprang to her feet
and began running away. However she seemed to be
weak or perhaps her stomach was too heavy with the
hens she had just eaten for she ran very slowly. The
farmer lunged at her and just barely missed catching her.
Which made him lunge after her again. And she just
barely avoided him again.

"I'll get you!" he roared. "Playing dead, eh? I'll get
you—you won't escape me!" And he raced after her.

But no matter how fast he ran, Mrs. Fox managed to
stay just ahead of his reach. Then, lo and behold, she
suddenly put on a burst of speed and fled for the woods.

The farmer, who had thought he would be able to
catch her, had left his gun behind. And now all he could
do was watch as she disappeared between the trees.

"Oh, you cunning fox!" he screamed. "But I'll fix you—
I'll make my hen house so strong that you'll never be
able to get into it again. Never, never . . . !"

But Mrs. Fox couldn't have cared less. At least not
until the farmer got some more hens. Because while she
had been drawing him away from his hen house, Mr. Fox
had marched through the open front door, as planned,
and carted off all the hens that were there.

The Most Worthy Boatman

Meet a man who does his job well—
Yes, extremely well indeed . . .

Many years ago there lived a boatman who made his home near a river.

Though there was a wooden bridge over this river, the boatman was still called upon quite often to take people across in his boat. You see, some people were too lazy to use the bridge when they wanted to get to the other side. And some people simply liked others to do things for them.

"Boatman, boatman," they would all call. "Take us across the river."

The boatman's work was hard and many times he was soaked through and through from the splashing waves. Nor did the people he took back and forth across the river make his job any more pleasant—they were not kind or considerate to him in the least. They seemed to feel that since there was a bridge they could always use, they were practically doing him a favor by letting him take them across. And they regarded him as hardly more than a servant. And paid him very little too.

Nevertheless, the boatman never complained. This was

47

the only work he had ever done or knew how to do. And he did it as best as he could.

One day as he was rowing some people across the river, the sky began to turn dark.

"Hurry, hurry!" his passengers demanded. "It's going to rain."

The boatman rowed as hard as he could. The skies grew darker.

Just as the first drops of rain began to fall, the boat touched shore. The people rushed ashore without so much as a thank you, even forgetting to pay the boatman in their haste to escape the rain.

The boatman just sighed and didn't complain. This had happened before. He was used to it by now.

Back across the river he rowed as the rain came down harder. When he reached the other shore a couple was waiting there for him to take them to the other side where they lived. He couldn't refuse.

So he began rowing them across as the rain came down harder and harder. And though they had been oh so nice to him when asking him to take them across, once under-way the couple huddled under their umbrella never so much as offering it as cover for him too, only urging him to go faster. When he reached the opposite shore, the couple tossed him a few coins and hurried off.

By the time the boatman had returned to the other side, the winds were howling and the rains were pouring down. Nobody was around which meant he could finally go home, for which he was very grateful. So he hurried to his house where he quickly lit a fire to dry himself and thaw the chill from his bones.

During the night the storm became worse. Through the darkness it howled like a thousand wolves and only as morning drew near did it begin to subside. Then with the break of dawn it was over.

When the boatman went outside, his eyes showed him what a ferocious storm it had been. The bridge across the river had been completely swept away. All that was left of it was a few splintered beams sticking up from the water.

People were lining the banks on both sides of the river wanting to cross to the opposite shores but unable to. As soon as they saw the boatman they began calling to him loudly: "Boatman, boatman, please take us across the river!"

So he loaded up his boat with as many people as he could and took them across to the far side of the river. Then he loaded up with as many people as he could from that side. Back and forth he went, taking as many people each trip as his boat would hold. His arms and back grew sore and stiff. But he never complained. This was his job and he would do it until it was done.

Finally there was only one boat load of people left on the far shore. He got them all into his boat and started out, his muscles so tired from rowing they were almost numb. But his poor boat was in even worse condition. The pounding it had taken from the storm and the heavy loads of people it had been forced to hold the past few hours had badly weakened its planks. The boat began to leak.

The boatman rowed with all his strength and just managed to touch shore before the boat began to sink. And in their rush to get out, the passengers kicked and banged the already battered bottom of the boat, pushing it through.

The boatman felt very bad. However, he was grateful

that he had been able to get so many people across the river before it had happened. In fact, there was only one person on this side of the river who wanted to cross—a young, handsome lad.

"I'm sorry," the boatman told him, "I crossed as many people as I could but now my boat is useless until it's repaired."

"So I see," said the young lad. "Can you take me across on your shoulders instead?"

"On my shoulders?" echoed the boatman. He had never thought of that. True, the river wasn't very deep but he was so tired. However there was only this one person left and such a little lad at that.

"Climb on," he said to him. And the lad climbed on his shoulders.

The boatman eased himself into the water, being very careful not to get the boy wet. He started wading across.

But with every step he took, the young lad seemed to become heavier and heavier. The boatman gritted his teeth and kept going. The lad seemed to get heavier still. Finally, when the boatman felt he could not go a single step further he reached shore. With a groan of relief he set the young lad down.

"That was the hardest job I ever did," he confessed, wiping the sweat from his brow.

"Here is your payment," said the lad.

"Thank you," said the boatman. Then he saw that the lad had given him a solid gold coin. "Wait, you must have made a mistake," he told him. "This coin is worth many times my charge."

"No longer it isn't," replied the young lad. "For you have proven how truly worthy you are. And from now on all your passengers must pay you that much—and will

With every step he took, the young lad seemed to become heavier and heavier.

treat you with the respect you deserve too." Then, suddenly, he was gone.

After the boatman repaired his boat, he took the young lad's advice and began charging the full worth of a gold coin for each person he crossed. And, sure enough, the people paid it gladly and were even far kinder and more considerate to him than they had ever been.

Of course it is known to be a fact that the more money people pay for a service, the more importance they attach to it and the better they treat the person doing it. However, the boatman didn't know about this. Besides, he had decided that his good fortune was entirely due to the young lad he had taken across the river on his shoulders. For he believed that young lad was none other than the patron saint of the boatmen who had come to test him, and finding him worthy, had rewarded him. But, of course, that couldn't be true.

Or could it?

The Two Women and Their Sons

There were once two friends, one rich and the other poor.
But which was which?

There once were two women who were rather good friends despite being in quite different circumstances. You see, one of them was very wealthy and the other was poor. The very wealthy woman was named Maria Rosa. The other woman was named Maria Isabel. Each of them had one son.

Now, whenever Maria Rosa sold her fruits and vegetables she would go to Maria Isabel's house and say:

"Oh, dear Maria Isabel—please ask your son to come to my house and add up the money I got today and let me know what the total is." For she wanted to know how much profit she had made and she had never bothered to learn how to add or otherwise use numbers. And her son, being the son of a wealthy woman, had also never bothered to learn how to use numbers. But Maria Isabel's son had learned how to use numbers.

So Maria Isabel would ask her son to please help Maria Rosa and he would do as she asked.

But that was not all. Oh, no.

Whenever Maria Rosa ordered fertilizer for her land
and she received word that it was arriving she would go
to Maria Isabel's house and say:

"Oh, dear Maria Isabel—the fertilizer I ordered for my
land is arriving at the post office this afternoon and I
wonder if you would please ask your son if he would
go there and get it for me." For a wealthy woman certainly could never be bothered picking up fertilizer. As
for her son, being the son of a wealthy woman, picking
up fertilizer was beneath him also. But it was not beneath Maria Isabel's son.

So Maria Isabel would ask her son to please pick up the
fertilizer at the post office for Maria Rosa and he would
do as she asked.

But that was not all either.

Whenever Maria Rosa wanted to write letters to anyone she would go to Maria Isabel's house and say:

"Oh, dear Maria Isabel—I need to send out a few letters today and I was wondering whether you would be
good enough to ask your son to write them for me." For
she had never bothered to learn how to write. And her
son, being the son of a wealthy woman, had also never
bothered to learn how to write. But Maria Isabel's son had
learned how to write.

So Maria Isabel would ask her son to please write some
letters for Maria Rosa and he would do as she asked.

But that was not all either.

One day Maria Rosa came to Maria Isabel's house and
said that her son was ill. And she asked Maria Isabel to
please ask her son to read the instructions on the bottles
of medicine she had gotten for him. For she had never
even bothered to learn how to read. And her son, being

So Maria Isabel would ask her son to please write some letters for Maria Rosa and he would do as she asked.

the son of a wealthy woman, had also never bothered to learn how to read.

So Maria Isabel asked her son to please read the instructions on the bottles of medicine Maria Rosa had so she would know how much of them to give to her son. And Maria Isabel's son did as she asked.

But when Maria Rosa had left, Maria Isabel's son shook his head sadly.

"It just isn't fair, mother," he said. "Your friend Maria Rosa is here practically every day asking me to either add up the money she's made or to get her fertilizer at the post office or to write letters for her. And today I even had to read the instructions on the medicine bottles for her so she would know how much medicine to give her son. She is always asking us for something or other. Yet she is so rich and you are poor—it just isn't fair."

Maria Isabel smiled. "So you think she is rich and I am poor? Oh, that is not quite true, my son. Go ask the people in the village who they think is richer, Maria Rosa or I. See what they have to say."

Maria Isabel's son was sure his mother must be mistaken. But he went to do as she had bid him.

"Who is richer—Maria Rosa or Maria Isabel?" he asked the first villager he met.

"Why, Maria Isabel, of course," came the answer.

Puzzled, the son continued on.

"Who is richer—Maria Rosa or Maria Isabel?" he asked the next villager he met.

"Maria Isabel, certainly," came the reply.

And the next person the son asked had the same answer. And the next person too. In fact, everybody he asked seemed to think that his mother was richer than Maria Rosa.

Very puzzled, he returned home.

"Everyone I asked thought you were richer than Maria Rosa," he told his mother. "I do not understand. Why does everybody think that?"

"Because it is so," answered his mother smilingly. "For I have a son who can read and write and do much more besides. While Maria Rosa's son can neither read nor write nor do much of anything. All Maria Rosa has is money. And everyone knows that money is of small value compared with a worthy son."

That, indeed, was the truth. Whether Maria Rosa knew it or would even admit it if she did, everyone else in the village knew it without a doubt.

The Queen of the Wolves

She was the cleverest of all creatures—
So she thought!

In the days when there were many wolves in Portugal
they were the proudest of all animals. They not only
thought they were the biggest and strongest creatures in
the world but also the smartest as well.

There was one wolf in particular who was even prouder
than the rest of her kind. Before leaving her cave she
would smooth her fur and make sure she looked as
pretty and fine as could be. And wherever she went
she walked with her head held high to show everybody
who saw her how grand she was.

Of course, the other animals around beside wolves were
much smaller than she was and feared her very much.
So it was really no great accomplishment for her to impress any of them—they were already so impressed by
fear that they wouldn't even show themselves whenever
they knew she was about.

In fact, the only creature that wasn't particularly impressed by her was man. Therefore, she was especially
anxious to impress men. Whenever she saw them working

in the fields she would go by them holding her head and tail as high as she could, trying with every step to show them just how regal she was.

As time passed, this wolf grew so proud of herself that she began to feel that she was too good to even eat the same old creatures she had always dined on. So one day she decided to find something for her dinner which she felt was truly worthy of a queen such as she. And off she went.

The first creature she came upon was a mouse.

"Oh, please don't eat me!" squeaked the mouse. He knew only too well that many of his relatives had been made into quick meals by wolves and he was half scared out of his wits that he was about to become one of those meals himself.

But the wolf just stuck her nose in the air and ignored him.

"I can certainly find something better to eat than a mouse," she sniffed. And she paraded right by.

The mouse was thankful as could be and hurried to get as far away as he could lest this wolf change her mind.

The wolf sauntered on, nose in the air. "How grand I am," she thought. "I am truly the greatest of all creatures."

Then she came upon a rabbit.

The rabbit was petrified with fear. "Oh, please, please don't eat me," he squealed. He well knew about the many other rabbits that had been made into meals by wolves and he was terrified that the same fate was about to be his too.

But the wolf didn't pay him the slightest attention.

"I can certainly find something better to eat than a rabbit," she sniffed. And she paraded right by.

The rabbit was as relieved as could be and scampered for his home as fast as he could.

The wolf marched on. "How grand I am," she thought. "I am surely the greatest of all creatures."

Suddenly she came upon a pheasant.

"Oh, oh, oh!" gasped the pheasant. For he knew what wolves did to pheasants and could just imagine what was in store for him.

But the wolf paid him no heed.

"I can certainly find something better to eat than a pheasant," she sniffed. And she sauntered right by.

The pheasant thanked his lucky stars and ran for his home as fast as he could.

The wolf continued on. "Ah, yes, how grand I am," she thought. "I am positively the greatest of all creatures."

Suddenly she heard a rustling in a nearby tree. Ever so quietly she inched toward it. . . . And then she saw him— an owl on one of the branches.

"Ah, this is indeed a meal fit for a queen," she said to herself, licking her chops.

She crouched low and then gave a mighty spring, catching the owl in her mouth.

The poor owl quaked with terror. Any second he could imagine the wolf's teeth closing together and ending his life. Nevertheless, he sought to gather his wits and see if there was any way he could save himself.

"Oh, great wolf, you have caught me fair and square," he declared. "May I make a feast worthy of such a great queen as you."

The wolf was so pleased by this compliment that she held off beginning her dinner to hear if the owl had any more such pretty words for her ears.

"Even men would be impressed by your having cap-

And she sauntered right by.

tured me," continued the owl. "For men think that owls are among the wisest of animals and if they learn you have caught me they will think that you must be even wiser."

The wolf was as pleased as could be. Yes, how she wished men knew she had caught the owl for her dinner. Then they, too, would realize she was the greatest of all creatures.

"Look, there are some farmers in the valley," said the owl. "You can tell them yourself you have caught me."

The proud wolf opened her mouth to do just that. But the second she did the owl was free and off he flew.

The wolf had been tricked. There would be no owl for her dinner that day. Moreover, word had quickly spread that the wolf was out hunting, so every other creature in the area had gone into hiding. Now the wolf could find nothing to eat.

It is said that the owl told the farmers the whole story of what had happened and they had a good, long laugh at the wolf's expense. And from that day on men looked upon owls as the wisest of all creatures with wolves far, far behind.

Some people say this so embarrassed the wolves that most of them left Portugal and that is why there are so few of them left there today. As for the few that are left, they stay in the mountains and rarely let themselves be seen by anyone.

The Poor Shoemaker

A gift of gold would surely make any poor man happy.
Well, not always . . .

Once there lived a poor shoemaker who had a wife and
many children. All day long he worked hard repairing
shoes for his customers. Though he never made much
money he did manage to make enough to feed and clothe
his family. And every evening after supper he would take
out his old guitar and play a few songs for his family
before the children's bedtime. Yes, poor as they were,
they found happiness in the little they had.

Now, it so happens there was a rich man in the village
who noticed how hard the poor shoemaker worked and
that he never made enough money to buy more than the
bare necessities of life. The rich man took pity on him
and one evening he went to the shoemaker's house and
gave him a bag of gold.

"This is for you," he said. "I notice how hard you work
and how little you have. So I want you to have this to
spend in any way that you like, to make your days a bit
happier."

The poor shoemaker was delighted. He thanked the

rich man a dozen times. Then he ran to his wife to
show her what they had gotten.

"Look, look what the rich man gave us!" he cried with
happiness. "All ours to spend on anything we wish!"

His wife was as excited by the gold as he was and they
spent many minutes just staring at it and letting it run
through their fingers. Then they begun to wonder what
they would buy.

They thought of many things they could buy with the
gold. Many, many things. But well past their bedtime
they had still not decided what to spend the gold on.

"It's very late," realized the shoemaker. "We'll just have
to decide tomorrow."

"All right," said his wife. "But where shall we keep
the gold tonight? I'm so afraid we might be robbed."

They thought and thought.

"Let's hide it under our bed," declared the shoemaker.

"Good idea," agreed his wife.

So they hid the gold under their bed and went to sleep.
But they did not sleep well at all. Whenever they closed
their eyes they wondered if the gold was still safe. Six
times the shoemaker opened his eyes and felt under the
bed to make sure the gold was still there. The seventh
time he opened his eyes to check his gold again, dawn
was breaking—it was time to get up.

The tired shoemaker went to his shop and started his
day's work. But his thoughts were on gold not work. He
kept thinking and thinking what he could buy with the
gold. Twice he banged his thumb instead of the shoe nails
he was aiming at and once he found himself hammering
a heel into place where a sole belonged.

When it was time for him to close his shop for the day

he hurried home as fast as he could. His wife had told the children about the gold and they excitedly greeted him with many suggestions as to what should be bought with it. His wife had a few more suggestions as well.

During supper they discussed the suggestions. And after supper too. In fact that's all they did was talk about what they should buy, right up until the time the shoemaker insisted that the children should have been asleep long ago and they should get to bed immediately.

When they had been tucked in bed, and had finally stopped crying, the shoemaker and his wife thought about where they should hide the gold for the night.

"I don't like putting it under our bed," said the shoemaker. "Anybody could sneak into the house while we're sleeping and make off with it in a second."

"How true," agreed his wife. "Perhaps we should bury it deep in the back yard. That way if anyone tried to steal it we would certainly hear the sounds of them digging in time to get help."

"Good thinking," said the shoemaker. So he buried the bag of gold deep in their back yard while his wife kept watch to make sure that no one was around. Then they went to bed.

But they slept no better than they had the night before. At every murmur of the wind they imagined there were robbers in the back yard digging for their gold. Six times the shoemaker raced to his window in alarm only to find that the yard was deserted. The seventh time he raced to the window he still found nobody there, except the sun coming up. So it was time for them to get up too.

Off went the very tired shoemaker to work. But his

*So he buried the bag of gold deep in their back yard while
his wife kept watch to make sure that no one was around.*

thoughts were on the gold. During the day he managed to put two soles on backwards and bang both his thumbs black and blue.

As soon as he could close his shop he dashed for home. He had thought of some wonderful new ways to spend the gold and he was anxious to tell his wife. But his wife had been thinking of new ways they could spend the gold too. And so had all the children.

During supper they argued over their suggestions, hardly knowing what they were eating. And after supper they continued the argument, coming up with more ideas as well.

It was long past the children's bed time before the shoemaker and his wife could get them tucked in. And when they finally stopped crying it was so late that the shoemaker and his wife could hardly stay awake any longer themselves. But before going to bed they had a problem to solve—where to put the gold for the night. They were afraid to keep it under their bed and they were afraid to bury it outside in their yard. But they didn't know where else to put it.

Finally they decided to keep it under their bed half the night and bury it in the yard the other half, so as to confuse any robbers who were planning to look for it. Which, they both agreed, was a wise idea.

But between changing the gold around in the middle of the night and checking every few minutes to make sure it was still safe—sometimes even forgetting which place it was in—they got less sleep than they ever had. In the morning the shoemaker and his wife were so exhausted they could hardly climb out of bed.

It was Sunday, the day of rest. But there was little rest at the shoemaker's house. For the shoemaker had more

ideas about how the gold should be spent. And so did his
wife. And so did each one of their children.

They argued all day long and right through supper
time. In fact they would have still been arguing except
the shoemaker left the house after supper. He went
straight to the rich man's house.

"I wish to return your gold to you," the shoemaker
said to him. "I don't want it. Please take it back." And he
held out the bag of gold to him.

The rich man was shocked. But there was nothing he
could do but take back his gold.

The shoemaker returned to his house. And there was
no more worrying about where to hide gold. Or suggestions and arguments about how it should be spent.

The shoemaker concentrated on making good shoes for
his customers. And putting soles and heels where they
belonged. And not banging his thumbs.

Once more he began playing the guitar after supper.
And his family all got to bed on time. And slept well.

And these were the only riches the shoemaker and his
family ever wanted again.

The Old Man and the Thieves

Two thieves learn a lesson.
And an old man learns one too . . .

One morning an old man with a donkey came traveling
down a dusty road on his way to the market place. The
donkey was carrying two jars of olive oil which the old
man had made and was taking to the market place to
sell, as he did every week. Over the donkey's head was
a halter with blinders to keep him from seeing off to
either side and thus being tempted to stray off his course,
as he often liked to do. The old man walked along beside
him, pulling at the rope on his halter to keep him from
stopping, as the donkey often liked to do also.

Along the way they approached two students heading
for their homes.

Now, these two students were not good boys. Not at
all. For the moment they saw the old man with the
donkey coming down the lonely road they decided to
steal the donkey from him. So they stepped out in front
of the donkey and the old man, forcing them to stop.

"Hold up there," said one of the students.

"What for?" said the old man.

"For this," said the other student. And he grabbed the rope of the donkey's halter from him. Then the two students began leading the donkey away.

The old man was stunned. He needed his donkey to take his olive oil to sell in the market place every week so he could make enough money to feed and clothe himself. How could he live without his donkey?

"Wait—please don't take my donkey!" he cried. But neither the students nor the donkey so much as even slowed down. They continued right on and were soon lost from sight.

The old man sat down by the side of the road and buried his head in his arms. He was too old to chase the thieves and even if he could catch them he knew he was too weak to ever get the donkey away from them. What could he do?

Finally the old man realized that his only hope was to go and explain his plight to the man who had named him godfather of his son a few years ago. For it was a big honor in Portugal to be named a godfather, and certainly his *compadre*,[1] who had given him such an honor, was the person to see now in his time of need.

So the old man went to him and told him what had happened.

"Could I please borrow some money from you to buy another donkey?" he asked. "I will be glad to pay you back a little each week from the money I receive for my olive oil."

To this his *compadre* agreed and gave him the money he requested.

So the old man thanked him very warmly and started out for the market place to buy another donkey. When he

---

1. *the father of your godchild*

arrived there who do you think he saw? Yes, the two students with his donkey and olive oil! They had taken a space in the market place, just as everyone else did who had something to sell, and were trying to persuade everybody who passed their way to buy their stolen goods.

Now, the students saw the old man too but they failed to recognize him. Perhaps it was because he looked so much like many of the other old men browsing through the things for sale in the market place. Or perhaps it was simply because they were too concerned with trying to sell the donkey and the olive oil. But the old man recognized them immediately. And his first thought was to yell out to everyone what thieves they were.

Then he realized they would probably be quick to deny everything; and since he was so old, they might well shout him down and convince the other people there that he was mistaken or even crazy. Besides, he saw they had not recognized him. That gave him an idea.

As he approached them the students called to him to come see the fine donkey they had for sale, as they were calling to everybody else nearby.

"May I inspect him?" asked the old man.

"Yes, of course," answered the two students. "See for yourself what a fine donkey he is."

The old man smiled and inspected him. Suddenly he spoke out in a loud voice:

"Whoever doesn't know you should buy you!" he said.

"Did you hear that?" declared a man nearby.

"Yes, did you hear that?" echoed another.

"He said whoever doesn't know that donkey should buy him," said a third man. "That means whoever knows him would not buy him."

"Whoever doesn't know you should buy you!" he said.

"There must be something very wrong with him," said another man.

"Yes, positively there must be," agreed a few more.

"Those two boys selling him must be trying to cheat us," declared a voice in the crowd. Soon everyone in the market place was talking about it. And the more they thought about it the surer they were that the two students were trying to sell them a sick or worthless donkey. And the angrier they became.

Finally they got so angry that they gave the two students a good beating and drove them away. So all those two ended up with for their thieving ways were several large lumps and bruises.

"These are mine," said the old man, claiming the two jars of olive oil. "Those two students stole them from me." And since there was no one around to dispute him he had no problem taking them.

As for the donkey, it had fled at the first outburst of trouble. The old man started to go after him. Then he changed his mind.

His donkey had never been a good donkey, he realized. Why, how many times had he been forced to pull and plead with his donkey to get him to do any work? And had his donkey so much as even tried to resist when the two students had taken him?

No, that was not the kind of donkey he wanted. He had the money now to buy himself a really good donkey —one he could trust and love who would love him in return and do his work willingly and well. That's the kind of donkey he would get.

And that's just the kind of donkey he did get.

The Ferocious Lark

A lark is only a very small bird.
But how ferocious she can be . . .

In the southern part of Portugal there lived a very rich
man. Like most rich men he owned a great deal of land.
And like most rich land owners he was always buying
more land whenever he could, then clearing it away to
raise crops on or to rent.

Everyone who knew him regarded him as very wise
to have accumulated so much money and land. People
congratulated him often. Sometimes he even congratulated himself. Sometimes he even liked to tease his wife
a little.

"You didn't marry badly, did you, my dear?" he would
say to her with a smile. "Have I not provided well for
you?"

"Yes, you have, my husband," she would answer. And
being a good wife that was all she said.

Other times he would say to her: "Are you not proud of
your husband? Am I not wiser than anyone you know?"

"Yes, you are, my husband," she would answer. And
being a good wife that was all she said.

The rich man bought more and more land. And he

74

hired more and more men to work for him. And he continued to tease his wife every so often too.

One morning he sent two of his farm hands to clear the brush and trees from a piece of land he had just bought, and that afternoon went out to see it to decide what he would plant there. But much to his surprise he discovered that the land had not yet been cleared.

He quickly returned to his house and ordered the men he had sent to clear that land to be brought before him.

"Why didn't you carry out my instructions?" he demanded of them.

The two farm hands looked at one another sheepishly and scratched their heads.

"We started to but something stopped us," said the first man.

"It was a bird," said the second man. "A lark. It flew around our heads when we approached your land and began pecking at us. It wouldn't let us go to work."

"A bird, a little lark wouldn't let you do your work?" the rich man repeated. He could hardly believe his ears. "Go, out of my sight!" he ordered them.

Then he called for his foreman.

"Send me five of our best men," he commanded him. "And make sure they are not afraid of birds," he sneered.

The foreman did as he was bid. When the five men he had chosen appeared before the rich man he ordered them to clear that piece of land right away. Off they went to do his bidding.

The next morning the rich man went out to that land again to decide what to plant there. But, much to his surprise, he found it had still not been cleared.

He rushed to his house and ordered the men who had been sent to clear the land brought before him.

"What happened?" he thundered at them. "Why isn't that land cleared?"

The five men hung their heads.

"We tried," they explained. "But there were too few of us. When we began to go to work this lark suddenly threw herself in our midst, pecking at us right and left. We tried to drive her off but we couldn't. Every time we tried to hit her, all we hit was the air."

"Out, out of my sight!" roared the rich man.

When they had gone he called his foreman before him.

"First thing tomorrow morning get all my workers, every one of them, and send them to clear that land!" he demanded. "I want you to report here to me at noon and I want that land completely cleared when you do. Do you understand?"

The foreman replied that he did and promised that he would personally see to it that the land was cleared before noon. And the following morning at dawn he gathered together all the workers, armed them with clubs, and marched them off to clear the land.

At noon the foreman reported back to his master. He was covered with lumps and bruises.

"Well, tell me that land is finally cleared," said the rich man.

"I can't," said the foreman.

"What?" cried the rich man.

"We tried, we tried but we couldn't," whined the foreman. "As we approached, the lark came diving to attack us. She seemed to be everywhere at once. Whenever we swung our clubs at her she seemed to be somewhere else. We kept swinging and swinging at her but all we managed to hit was each other."

And being a good wife, that was all she said.

The rich man heaved a sigh. Shaking his head in defeat he dismissed his foreman.

"I don't know what to do," he told his wife that evening during supper. "That new piece of land I just bought must be guarded by the most ferocious lark in the world. It won't let any of my men by to clear the land for planting. I'm afraid we'll never be able to use it."

"Oh, I'm sure everything will turn out all right," said his wife. "Just leave the lark alone for a few days and it will soon be gone. Then you will be able to do whatever you wish with that land."

"How I only wish it," sighed her husband, dismissing her words as merely a woman's idle chatter.

But a few days later a strange thing happened: one of his workers reported that he had just noticed the lark flying off into the distance followed by four of the tiniest larks he had ever seen.

The rich man immediately ordered his foreman to try to clear the new piece of land again. And within an hour it had been done without the slightest bit of trouble.

That night the rich man could not refrain from asking his wife how she had known the lark would be leaving.

"It was not hard," she explained. "Any creature that would try so desperately to keep you off that land could only be protecting a new family. And as soon as her young ones were old enough to fly she would certainly lead them away from danger."

Now the rich man understood.

"I am even wiser than I thought to have married a woman as wise as you," he smiled.

"If you say so, my husband," she answered. And being a good wife, that was all she said.

The Seven Sons

A father teaches his sons a lesson—
One worth remembering all their lives . . .

There was an old man with seven sons who had come to the end of his days. As he lay in his bed slipping toward his eternal rest, he realized there was one more thing he wanted to do before it was time for him to depart. So he called his seven sons to his bedside and asked each of them to bring him a branch from a tree.

They immediately went to do his bidding and when they had returned with the branches they had found, he called the oldest son to his side.

"Give me your branch," he said to him.

When the oldest son gave it to him he handed it to the youngest son who was only seven years old.

"Try to break it," the father told him.

Without any trouble the little lad did.

"Now break this one," the father told him, giving him the second son's branch.

And the youngest son did.

"Now break this one," the father told him, giving him the third son's branch.

And the youngest son did.

"Try to break it," the father told him. Without any trouble the little lad did.

"Now break this one," the father told him, giving him the fourth son's branch.

And the youngest son did.

"Now break this one," the father told him, giving him the fifth son's branch.

And the youngest son did.

"Now break this one," the father told him, giving him the sixth son's branch.

And the youngest son did.

"Now break your own branch," the father told him.

And the youngest son did.

"Now, each of you bring me another branch," the father said to his sons.

Surprised by his odd requests, but obedient to his wishes as always, they went to do his bidding. When they returned, the father told the oldest son to take all the branches and tie them together.

"Now try to break them," the father said to him.

The oldest son tried but he couldn't.

"Try harder," said the father.

The oldest son tried again with all his strength. But he still couldn't.

'No, I can't break them, Father," he said.

"Then you and my second son try to break them," said the father.

So the two sons tried together to break the bundle of branches. But they couldn't.

"Then you two and my third son together try to break them," said the father.

So the three sons tried together. But they couldn't.

"Then you three and my fourth son together try to break them," said the father.

So the four sons tried together. But they couldn't.

"Then you four and my fifth son together try to break them," said the father.

So the five sons tried together. But they couldn't.

"Then you five and my sixth son together try to break them," said the father.

So the six sons tried together. But they couldn't.

"Then all of my sons, the seven of you together, try to break them," said the father.

So they all tried together. But they still couldn't.

Then the father separated the branches and gave them to the youngest son. "Now break them one by one," he told him.

And the youngest son easily broke them one at a time.

"Do you see what you have learned here, my sons?" said the father. "Even the youngest and weakest among you can break these branches when they are separated. But not all of you together can break them when they are united. And the same that is true of branches is true of people. Separated in the world they are only weak and vulnerable. But united they are strong and invincible. Remember this lesson well, my sons. It is the most valuable thing I can leave with you."

The sons did remember it well. In everything they did they stayed united, and as a result became the most powerful force in the village. And they earned for themselves much respect and riches as well.

Other families learned this lesson too. And it is a lesson worth repeating. So there could be more such families. Maybe yours.

The Great Antonio

He was the most famous of all street singers—
But nobody could understand why . . .

In olden days there were many men who used to sing for
their living. They would go traveling from village to village, stopping at each one to sing a few songs and collect
the few coins that the villagers would give them in return. Then on they would go to the next village.

Now, most of these traveling singers were very poor.
The money they received in return for their songs was
just about enough to keep body and soul together. Except
for one singer. He did quite well for himself. Yes, quite
well indeed. In every village he got two or three times as
many coins as any other singer received. In fact he even
had a helper who would precede him into the village to
put up signs announcing his coming. And when he arrived, this helper would announce that too, beating on a
drum and calling:

"The Great Antonio is here! Gather around . . . here is
the Great Antonio!"

The villagers would flock to hear him. And when Antonio finished singing, he would tell them a few words
of his philosophy about life and living. Then, when he

The villagers would flock to hear him.

was through, the villagers would show their appreciation with a shower of coins. In every village Antonio went the same thing happened—the people would listen to his singing and philosophy and then shower him with coins, far more than they gave to any other of his kind.

The other traveling singers could not figure out why Antonio made so much more money than they did. At first they felt it might be because of his views on life and living which he told to the people after he sang. But when they tried the same thing it won them no more coins than they ever got. In fact, in some cases their listeners would show signs of boredom and even walk away. So they begrudgingly conceded that the reason for Antonio's success must be that the villagers simply liked his singing. But none of them would ever admit that Antonio was a better singer than he was. In fact, there was only one of the traveling singers who admitted that there was anything special about Antonio's voice at all. That was Antonio himself.

"I am the best singer in the world," he would proudly say in explaining his success. "And the villagers respect my philosophy too. That is why they give me so much money."

Antonio's fellow singers would just shrug their shoulders and say nothing. There was nothing they could say.

As time passed, Antonio became prouder and prouder of himself. He told his helper to beat the drum more loudly when he made his appearance and cry out his name more loudly too. This his helper did.

"Here comes Antonio!" he would cry loudly. "The Great Antonio has arrived—he is here!"

The people would come from every corner of the vil-

lage. Then Antonio would grandly step out into the street
and bow to them with a flourish.

"Here I am," he would announce. "Gather around me,
my people."

Then he would sing. Then he would speak. Then the
people would shower him with coins.

And the prouder Antonio became, the more pains he
began to take in his philosophy. He began to think for
long stretches at a time, carefully preparing his ideas
before speaking, striving to make them as important as
he could. He even began to ponder the hows and whys
of creation.

And the people listened to him and showered him with
money.

In a village one day, he told how he had recently sat
under an enormous oak tree and a tiny acorn had fallen
from it, hitting his hand. And he went on to say that he
had then observed many small plants on the ground with
large pumpkins growing on them.

"Right away I could see there was something wrong
with this," Antonio declared to his audience. "Why did
the Creator ever give the tiny acorns to the big oak tree
and the huge pumpkins to the small plants? I would have
done it the other way around—put the big pumpkins on
the oak tree and the little acorns on the small plants.
That would have made far more sense."

And the people listened to him and showered him with
money.

But Antonio's helper happened to notice one man who
did not throw Antonio any money at all.

"Why do you not give money to the Great Antonio?"
he asked.

"Because he talks nonsense, that's why," the man answered. "If the Creator had put pumpkins where the acorns were, can you imagine the lumps and bruises people would get from pumpkins falling on them instead of acorns? And can you imagine how much harder it would be for a hungry traveler to satisfy his appetite if such delicious fruit as pumpkins grew high on oak trees instead of on the ground?"

"What is your name?" Antonio's helper asked him.

"José," came the reply.

"Can you sing?" asked Antonio's helper.

"A little," he replied.

"That will do," said Antonio's helper. Antonio could hardly sing and it had never mattered. This José was right, Antonio had been giving the people a lot of nonsense lately. It was due to the swelled head he was getting, that was the reason. Why, Antonio was even acting as if he really believed his singing and philosophy were responsible for his success. He was almost forgetting who and what made villagers think he was so great.

Yes, this José seemed like a good replacement indeed, Antonio's helper realized. Yes, it was time for a new star to be born—time for he and his drum to bid good-bye to the Great Antonio and bring on the Great José.

The Tablecloth, the Cow and the Club

Three brothers set out to find their fortunes—
And what strange fortunes they each found . . .

Many days ago there lived a builder who had three sons.
And the time came when the eldest son wanted to go out
and make his own fortune in the world. So, with his
father's blessing, off he went.

After traveling for two days he encountered a stranger
on his way to the next town. They struck up a conversa-
tion and agreed to journey together for a while.

When it began to get dark the stranger suggested they
pause in their travels to eat. To this the eldest son agreed.

The stranger took a tablecloth from his knapsack and
placed it on the ground.

"Make yourself, tablecloth," he said. And, lo and behold, the tablecloth was suddenly covered with food.

Never before had the eldest son seen such a marvelous
thing.

After eating, he and the stranger continued on and then
parted at a crossroads to go their separate ways. But the
eldest son had not gone far when he heard savage howls
from the direction in which he had just come. Racing

"Make yourself, tablecloth," he said.

back along the path he discovered the stranger surrounded by attacking wolves.

Immediately the eldest son threw himself into the center of them. And striking left and right with great bravery and strength he finally managed to kill them all.

The stranger was so grateful to him that he gave him the magic tablecloth.

The eldest son thanked him many times and then headed for home with the tablecloth as fast as he could. When he arrived home he showed it to his father and told him everything that had happened.

His father was very proud of him and praised him on his bravery that had brought him such good fortune.

"You did a fine deed and you were blessed with a great reward. Congratulations, my son."

When the second son heard about this he too was anxious to go out in the world and see what fortune he could find. So, after obtaining his father's blessing, off he went.

After traveling for two days he encountered an old man with a cow. And since they were both headed in the same direction they decided to continue on together. Soon they had become good friends.

When they reached a fork in the road where the old man went to turn off for his home, they parted with a handshake and headed on their separate ways. But the second son had not gone far when he heard the sounds of a violent struggle behind him. He raced back the way he had come to find the old man surrounded by a band of thieves.

Throwing himself upon them he fought like ten men and succeeded in sending them fleeing.

The old man was so grateful that he insisted the second son take his cow as a reward.

"This is a very special cow," he explained. "She gives money instead of milk. Just ask her for some, you'll see."

Sure enough, when the second son asked the cow for some silver coins they came falling out of her mouth.

The second son thanked the old man gratefully and then started for home with the cow as fast as he could. When he arrived home he showed it to his father and told him everything that had happened.

His father was very proud of him and praised him on his bravery that had brought him such good fortune.

"You did a worthy deed and were blessed with a splendid reward. Congratulations, my son."

When the youngest son heard about this he too was anxious to go out into the world to see what his fortune would be. However, since he was quite young and much smaller than his brothers, his father was reluctant to let him go. Besides, his father did not think he was even as smart as his brothers, certainly not smart enough to be off on his own yet and face the ways of the world. Nevertheless the youngest son persisted so the father finally gave in. And off the youngest son went.

He had been traveling for two days when he, too, met a stranger. And since they were both going in the same direction they went on together.

But they had not gone far when they were attacked by the same band of thieves that the second son had driven off just a few days ago. And since the thieves were still sore from the beating they had suffered that day, they were in an ugly mood and out to have their revenge.

The youngest brother tried to help the stranger fight them off but they were too much for him.

Just as the situation was becoming desperate, the stranger reached for his club.

"Strike, club, strike!" he said to it. And, lo and behold, the club began beating the thieves soundly. One by one they fell lifeless to the ground until they were all dead.

"Oh, what a remarkable club that is!" exclaimed the youngest son. "Can I buy it from you?"

Since all the thieves were dead, the traveler realized he probably would not need it again on the rest of his journey. So he decided to sell it to the youngest son.

"I'll sell it for all the money you have," he said.

The youngest son turned his pockets inside out and gave the stranger every last coin he had. Then he took the club and hurried for home as fast as he could.

When he arrived home he showed it to his father and told him everything that had happened.

However his father was anything but pleased. "What good is a club like that here?" he declared angrily. For the village where they lived had never been troubled by any thieves or bandits. "Leave it to you to waste all your money on something worthless. I should have known you were too young and foolish to go out on your own in the world yet."

As for the other two sons they were too concerned with their own affairs to pay any attention to their younger brother's return. There was to be a feast in their honor that evening to celebrate their good fortune and they were busy getting ready for it.

When they arrived at the feast they were in the best of spirits.

"Take good care of my tablecloth," said the eldest brother leaving it with the woman attendant. He had brought it to show off to everyone later. "Above all, don't say: 'Make yourself, tablecloth,' or strange things will happen," he told her with a proud smile. Then he went inside.

The second son left his cow with the woman attendant too. For he had brought it also to show off to everyone later.

"Take good care of my cow," he told her. "Above all, don't say: 'Make money for me, cow,' or strange things will happen," he told her with a grin. Then he went inside too.

Now, the lady the two brothers had left their treasured possessions with was usually very trustworthy. But their boastful words had so tempted her that she just had to try saying what they had told her not to say. And when she did, she saw just how wondrous the tablecloth and the cow were. So she hid them both, intent upon keeping them for herself.

When the brothers came back to claim their tablecloth and their cow she informed them they had somehow disappeared. And fuss as they might, the two brothers could not get anything further out of her. There was nothing they could do but return home in disgrace.

When their younger brother heard what had happened he hastily dressed and, taking his club, hurried to the feast. When he arrived, he gave his club to the woman attendant.

"Take good care of my club," he told her. "Above all, don't say: 'Strike, club strike,' or strange things will happen." Then he went inside.

As soon as he was gone the woman couldn't resist saying what he had told her not to say, to see if the club was as valuable and wonderful as the tablecloth and the cow. But as soon as she said: 'Strike, club, strike," the club began beating her.

"Help, help!" she cried.

The younger brother came rushing out.

"The club will not stop until you have told me where you have hidden the tablecloth and the cow," he said.

"I don't know, I don't know where they are!" cried the woman. But the club beat her harder and harder until she finally gave in and told the truth.

When the younger brother returned home with the tablecloth and the cow, needless to say his brothers were very grateful. Also needless to say, his father was very surprised. And though the father never admitted it, from that day on he realized that his youngest son was truly the wisest one of all.

The Stingy Neighbor

*Once there was a man determined not to share what he
had. Oh was he in for a surprise . . .*

In a village in Portugal there were two men who lived
right next to one another. Now, it was the custom in this
village—as it was in most villages in Portugal—that whenever anyone harvested or prepared a large amount of food
he would give a portion of it to the richest, most important person in his village.

The reason for this was that most Portuguese people
felt it was not only a good thing to do but a wise thing
as well to share what they had with their richest, most
important neighbor. It was like a sort of insurance in
case the time ever came that they needed something from
him.

Well, in this particular village the richest, most important person was a man by the name of Mr. Silva. Whenever anybody in the village gathered a crop of vegetables
he would set aside some of them to give to Mr. Silva.
Or whenever anybody slaughtered one of his pigs for a
feast he would set aside a shoulder of the pig to give
to Mr. Silva.

Now, it so happens that of the two men who lived

right next to each other in this village one of them was quite poor while the other was almost as rich as Mr. Silva. But the man who was almost as rich as Mr. Silva was very stingy. One day when he went to slaughter a pig of his for a feast he confessed to his poorer neighbor that he did not want to give a whole shoulder of the pig to Mr. Silva. In fact, he did not want to give Mr. Silva even the slightest part of his pig.

"Why should I give Silva any of my pig?" he complained. "Silva is much richer than I am. I can certainly use my pig better than he can."

His neighbor was shocked. "But it's the custom," he said. "What would everybody say if they heard you had killed a pig and not given a shoulder of it to Mr. Silva."

"Ah, but I have thought of a way that nobody will ever know," declared the stingy man. "After I kill my pig I will hang him outside to let him dry before stuffing. Then, in the middle of the night, I will sneak him into the house and tell everyone the next morning that he was gone when I awoke and he must have been stolen. That way nobody will know I still have him and I won't have to give Silva so much as a taste of him. Isn't that a brilliant idea?"

Well, his neighbor had to agree that it was indeed a clever way to keep Silva from getting any of the pig—he couldn't dispute that. So the stingy man gleefully went home and prepared to carry out his plan. He killed his pig and then hung him up outside his house that evening.

Just before dawn he awoke and quietly slipped from his house to sneak the pig inside. But, lo and behold, the pig was gone! He searched the grounds around his house in a frenzy but the pig was nowhere to be found.

And what a sumptuous meal they sat down to—a whole roast pig.

He dashed to the home of his neighbor.

"I've been robbed—I've been robbed!" he cried to him. "My beautiful pig has been stolen."

The neighbor tried to console him. "Well, at least there is one good thing about it," he said. "That story you were going to make up about your pig being stolen turned out to be the truth after all. Now you don't have to worry about anybody discovering that you didn't plan to give one of the pig's shoulders to Mr. Silva."

But the stingy man didn't feel any better. "I've been robbed—I've been robbed," he moaned over and over again. "A whole big, fat pig—stolen—gone!"

Finally, still moaning over his loss, he departed for home.

His neighbor watched him go then turned to his wife.

"This would never have happened if he had just given a shoulder of his pig to Mr. Silva as everybody else does," he said.

"That's true," agreed his wife, bringing their breakfast to the table. "Serves the old tightwad right for being so stingy."

And what a sumptuous meal they sat down to—a whole roast pig.

"Besides, we can certainly use it better than he can," they smiled.

And they didn't forget to save one of the shoulders for Mr. Silva.

The Remarkable Woman

There never was a woman any more wonderful
than this woman. There just couldn't be . . .

Once upon a time there lived a remarkable woman who
was known as Mae. She was so remarkable that everyone she worked for expected her to do everything they
asked of her without the slightest hesitation or complaint.
And she did.

In the morning she would awake at dawn and begin
preparing breakfast.

"More butter, more bread, Mae," the father of the
family would often demand of her when he sat down
to eat.

And Mae would rush to get him what he wanted.

"Mae, Mae—I can't find my socks," little brother would
often cry. Or sometimes it was his shoes. Or even his
shirt.

But, whatever it was, Mae would immediately hurry
to his room and search under the bed and in the corners
until she found what he was looking for.

"Mae, there's a button missing from my coat," big
sister would often call. "Come sew it on for me please.
Hurry, hurry or I'll be late for school."

And Mae would hurry to sew on the button. Or find her hair ribbon which she often misplaced. Or iron the blouse she wanted to wear right away.

Without a complaint or even a frown, Mae would do everything asked of her.

Then she would busy herself getting little brother and big sister off to school. And, when they were gone, she helped their father take his tools to the field. Then she would return to the house and begin to clean up the kitchen.

When she had finished in the kitchen, she made all the beds then did all the dusting. Then she began the mending—a pair of ripped trousers, two socks with holes in them and a torn shirt and blouse. Then she had to do the washing.

When she had finished with that it was time to prepare lunch for the father of the house and bring it to him. Which she did. Then she stayed with him for the afternoon, helping him do the planting and the cultivating and the pulling out of the weeds that threatened to choke the vegetables he was growing. She worked until her back ached. But she never complained.

When the children returned from school, as tired as she was she greeted them with a smile. Then began to prepare dinner. Then she helped them with their homework until it was time to eat.

After dinner she cleared the table, then washed the dishes, then finished some mending she had left over from the morning. Then she helped little brother get ready for bed. And told him a bedtime story until he drifted off to sleep.

Now, it may seem that everybody in this house expected a great deal from Mae and were even inclined to

Mae

take advantage of her. This is quite true. But it also so happens that they all loved her very much. In fact, they thought there was no one else in the world as wonderful as her.

But, you see, almost every family in Portugal had a Mae of their own who did practically everything that had to be done for them too. And each family felt there was nobody else in the world as wonderful as their own Mae.

Now, of course, they couldn't all be right. But, then again, no one could really call them wrong either.

For Mae is the word in Portuguese for Mother.